101 OUTER SPACE JOKES

by Sonia Black and Devra Newberger
illustrated by Ricky Mujica

SCHOLASTIC INC.
New York Toronto London Auckland Sydney

ISBN 0-590-42972-8

12 11 10   3 4/9

Printed in the U.S.A.   01

First Scholastic printing, September 1989

MARTIAN MADNESS

What did Elliott say when E.T. went home?

E.T. come, E.T. go!

Why does E.T. have such big eyes?

You would, too, if you saw his phone bill!

What comes from outer space and leads a parade?

A Martian band!

First Martian: That girl over there rolled her eyes at me. What should I do?

Second Martian: If you were a real gentleman, you'd pick them up and roll them back to her!

First Alien: I was born on Mars.

Second Alien: What part?

First Alien: All of me, of course!

The weary traveler went into a restaurant for dinner. There was a piano player entertaining the patrons. The weary traveler found the beautiful music very soothing.

As he intently watched the piano player, he suddenly saw an alien creature emerge from the top of the piano. The piano player kept on playing as though he was unaware of what was happening. The weary traveler stared in amazement. Another alien creature crawled out of the piano. Then another — and another. Still the piano player kept on playing as if nothing out of the ordinary was happening.

Finally the weary traveler went over to the piano player and asked, "Do you know four alien creatures just climbed out of your piano?"

"No," the piano player replied, "but if you hum a few bars, I can probably fake it!"

The space creature woke up in a terrible mood. He yelled at his wife, "Where's my food? . . . Where are my chains? . . . Where's my poison? Where is my — ?"

"Now wait just one minute," his wife replied. "Can't you see I've only got four hands?"

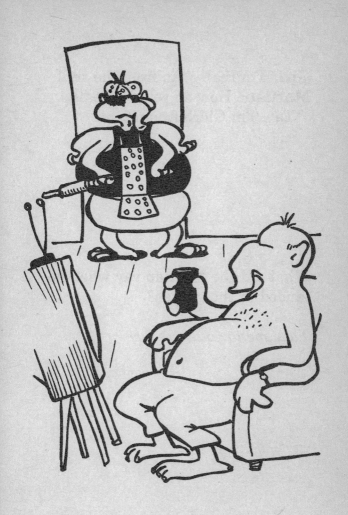

Girl: I'm really tan from the sun!
Martian: How do you do, Really
  Tan. I'm Glorb from Mars!

What did the Martian say when he
landed in the garden?

Take me to your weeder!

What do Martians have that no other creatures have?

Baby Martians!

Jim: What did the moon boy say to the moon girl?
Tim: Let's go for a walk. There's a beautiful earth out tonight!

Alien from Glorb: Are the creatures on your planet ugly?

Alien from Orb: Oh, yes. We just had a beauty contest recently and nobody won!

Billy: Why are you snapping your
 fingers like that?
Milly: To keep away monsters from
 outer space.
Billy: Outer-space monsters? I
 don't see any outer-space
 monsters around here.
Milly: See. It works!

What was E.T.'s favorite decade?

The 19ET's.

Three Martians went to a Masquerade Space Party on Jupiter. When they arrived at the party, one Martian was wearing false ears and eyebrows. "What have you come as?" asked the host. "Mr. Spock," replied the Martian. The second Martian was wearing black boots, black trousers, and a red jumper. "And what have you come as?" asked the host. "Scotty," replied the second Martian. The third Martian was dressed as a tree. "And what have you come as?" asked the host. "The Captain's Log," replied the Martian!

What do you do with a green alien?

Wait until it ripens.

How do you greet a two-headed alien?

Hello! Hello!

Harry: Imagine you were on Mars, surrounded by Martians. What would you do?

Larry: I would stop imagining!

"What steps would you take," asked the instructor of an astronauts' training course, "if enemy alien Martians came at you with laser weapons?"

A small, soft voice from the back of the room answered, "Great *big* ones, sir!"

Reporter: Professor, why did the alien spaceship land in New York City and take off so quickly?

Professor: It couldn't find a place to park!

First Scientist: Why do you think Martians have antennae?

Second Scientist: So they can watch their favorite TV shows like *Lost in Space* and *My Favorite Martian*!

Why did it take three hours for the Martian to finish a 20-page book?

It wasn't very hungry!

How do you talk to a giant Martian?

With big words!

Where do Martians leave their
spaceships when shopping?

At a parking meteor!

How do you get a Martian baby to
sleep?

You rocket (rock-it)!

What is a Martian's normal eyesight?

20–20–20–20–20–20– !

If a Martian spaceship carrying only Martians were to crash on Saturn, where would you bury the survivors?

You don't bury survivors!

Where are dead Martians listed?

In the orbit-uaries!

What did the Martian say to the
gasoline pump?

*Hey, take your finger out of your ear
and listen to me!*

How does an extraterrestrial count
to 19?

On one of its hands!

STAR STRUCK

Tim: Can you name a shooting star?

Jim: Sure, Clint Eastwood!

Son: Dad, I'd like to study the stars when I grow up.

Rich Dad: Certainly, son, and I'll buy Hollywood and Beverly Hills for you, too!

Nit: That star over there is Mars.

Wit: Then the other one must be Pa's!

What kind of star wears sunglasses and drives a Porsche?

A movie star!

Mamie: There's the Dog Star.
Amy: Are you Sirius?

What type of baseball game is held in a planetarium?

An all-star game!

Why did the astronomer hit himself
on the head in the afternoon?

*He wanted to see stars during the
day for a change!*

Girlfriend: What are you going to do tonight?

Astronomer: I'm going to Hollywood and watch the stars come out.

Nit: I'm going to cross a galaxy with a toad.

Wit: I wouldn't do that if I were you.

Nit: Why not?

Wit: Don't you know what you'll get?

Nit: No. What?

Wit: Star Warts!

Willie: I always wondered how
they put milk in the Milky Way.
Millie: With the Big Dipper!

Ilene: That's a comet.
Irene: A what?
Ilene: A comet, Irene. Don't you
know what a comet is?
Irene: No.
Ilene: Don't you know what they
call a star with a tail?
Irene: Sure. Mickey Mouse!

If the moon revolves around the
earth, and the earth revolves
around the sun, where are all the
stars?

In Hollywood!

LUNAR LOONINESS

Why couldn't the astronaut land on the moon?

Because it was full!

Teacher: Which is more important, the sun or the moon?
Student: The moon, because it shines at night when it's dark. The sun shines in the day, when it's light anyway!

Will: The moon is going broke.

Bill: Why do you say that?

Will: The TV weatherman says the
moon is down to its last quarter!

Teacher: As we have just learned,
the moon is round and hangs in
space without any support. Janey,
please tell the class how you can
prove it.

Janey: I don't have to prove it. I
never said that it does!

Earth: How are your craters?
Moon: Oh, they're depressed.

What beam weighs the least?

A moon beam!

What kind of insects live on the moon?

Lunar ticks (lunatics)!

Teacher: Why does it take over 72 hours to get to the moon?
Student: Because it's uphill all the way!

Ronald: Hey, did you hear the joke about the moon?

George: Yeah, it's far out!

Bill: I saw something last night that I couldn't get over!

Jill: What was it?

Bill: The moon!

Pam: How many balls of string
would it take to reach the moon?
Sam: Only one — one big one!

Wendy: Isn't it sad that you will never see a full moon again!

Wanda: Why not?

Wendy: Because the astronauts brought part of it back with them!

Who was the first man in space?

The man in the moon!

What kitchen utensil does the man in the moon never leave home without?

A cheese crater!

Why is the moon like a dollar?

Because it has four quarters!

What holds the moon up?

Moon beams!

SUN-SATIONAL
SILLINESS

What happens when the sun gets tired?

It sets awhile!

Did you hear the one about the man who stayed up all night, trying to figure out where the sun went when it went down?

It finally dawned on him!

Jill: I would love to travel to the sun.
Jack: You can't go to the sun; you'll burn up.
Jill: No, I wouldn't. I'd go at night!

Which is lighter, the sun or the earth?

The sun — it rises every morning!

What kind of bath can you take without water?

A sunbath!

Why is the sun like a black eye?

Because they are both shiners!

Who was the first settler in the West?

The sun!

How can you tune into the sun?

Turn its sundial!

What's the difference between the sun and a loaf of bread?

One rises from the east and the other from yeast!

PLANET CRACK-UPS

Jane: Do you think there is any intelligent life on Mars?

John: Sure, I do. You don't see them spending billions of dollars to come here, do you?

Saturn: I bet I get married before you do.

Venus: Why?

Saturn: Because I already have a ring.

Teacher: If people on Mars sent us a message, how could they tell if we received it?

Student: They could send it collect and see if we paid for it!

Bill: Do you know what a satellite is?

Phil: Sure. It's what you put on your horse if you're going to ride him after dark!

Which planet is the noisiest?

Saturn, because it has so many rings.

What's the best way to have a good space party?

Planet (plan it)!

Teacher: Robert, do you think there is life on Mars?
Robert: I don't know about Mars, but I can't even find a copy on my corner newsstand!

ASTRO-NUTTINESS

Mother: I think our son is going to be an astronaut.
Father: What makes you say that?
Mother: I spoke to his teacher today. She said he is taking up space!

Interviewer: Tell me, what is the secret of space travel?
Astronaut: Don't look down!

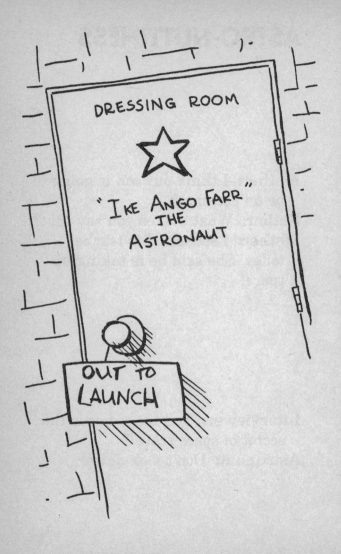

Sign on the astronaut's door:
OUT TO LAUNCH.

Astronaut: Did you see the
computer programmer?
Technician: She was right here,
but she just left.
Astronaut: Which way did she go?
Technician: She went data way.

What do you call a crazy spaceman?

An astro-nut!

What did the astronaut find in the
center of gravity?

The letter "V"!

During astronaut training class, the instructor turned to a student and said, "Belsky, imagine you are on a deserted planet and you're facing the North Star. Now, what is on your right?"

"East, sir," answered Belsky.

"That's right!" said the instructor. "And what is on your left?"

"West, sir."

"Right again! And what is at your back?"

"Um . . . my oxygen pack, I hope!"

If an athlete gets athlete's foot and a tennis pro gets tennis elbow, what does an astronaut get?

Missile toe!

A caravan of three spaceships took off to explore a remote, lifeless planet close to the sun. One of the spaceships crash-landed on the planet, damaging the ship, but leaving its four passengers unhurt.

The head astronaut instructed the other three astronauts to accompany him on the journey to seek help. The first astronaut took with him an umbrella, the second astronaut took with him a bottle, and the third astronaut removed the spaceship's door and carried it along with him. The four men set out to find help.

After a few hours of trudging across the hot, scorching planet, they stopped to rest. The leader turned to the first astronaut and asked, "Why did you bring an umbrella with you? There isn't any rain on this planet."

"It isn't to protect me from the rain," answered the astronaut. "It's to protect me from the sun's rays."

"Ah," replied the leader, "that makes good sense! And what about you?" he asked the second astronaut. "Why have you brought a bottle with you on this journey?"

"Why, this bottle is to keep us from dying of thirst!" answered the astronaut. "It is filled with water!"

"That also makes good sense!" said the leader. "But what about you?" he asked the third astronaut. "Why have you brought the spaceship's door with you on our quest for help?"

"Simple," answered the astronaut. "I, too, was worried about the heat. So I thought that if I carried the door and it got too hot, I could always roll down the window!"

What did the astronauts see in
their skillet?

An Unidentified Frying Object!

Why did Captain Kirk bring Wisk detergent to planet Saturn?

He wanted to get rid of the ring around the planet!

Why couldn't Captain Kirk smile?

Because Mr. Spock and Scotty were standing on the captain's bridge!

Why did Mr. Sulu bring antacid tablets with him to Jupiter?

Because he heard that the planet was filled with gas!

Where do astronauts keep their wallets?

In air pockets!

Flight Commander: Well, tomorrow's the big day — you'll be flying to the moon solo!
Astronaut: How low?

What does an astronaut do when he gets dirty?

He takes a meteor shower!

How is an escaping prisoner like an astronaut?

They both want safe flights and outer space!

Why did the young man become an astronaut?

Because everyone said he was no earthly good.

Who gets congratulated when they are down and out?

Astronauts!

ANIMALS IN SPACE

What dance steps can cows do on the moon?

The mooooon walk!

How did the cow jump over the moon?

She followed the milky way!

What do you call cattle battles in outer space?

Steer wars!

What do you call cattle who eat grass in space?

Star grazers!

Who was the first deer astronaut?

Buck Rogers!

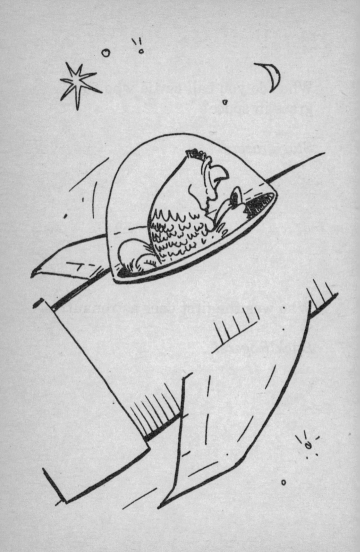

Who was the first chicken in space?

Cluck Rogers!

How did the baby lamb get to
Mercury?

By rocket sheep!

Why were Mickey Mouse and Goofy boarding the Space Shuttle?

Because they wanted to visit Pluto!

Why is a fat cow like a shooting star?

They are both meteor (meatier)!

When was beef the highest it's been?

When the cow jumped over the moon!

MISSILE-LANEOUS

How can you stop Darth Vader's forces from charging?

Take away their credit cards!

Teacher: A modern space shuttle can do anything that a bird can do and more!
Student: Oh, really. I'd like to see one of them lay an egg!

Knock, knock.
Who's there?
Athena.
Athena who?
Athena flying thaucer go by!

Joe: Can you telephone from a
spaceship?

Moe: Sure, I can tell a phone from
a spaceship!

What kind of dish is out of this
world?

A flying saucer!

What does Luke Skywalker shave
with?

A laser blade!

Some books to read in space:
Trying To Land Safely
   by Major Catastrophe
A Trip to Venus
   by Miles A. Waye
How To Become an Astronomer
   by I.C. Stars
Let's Fly to the Moon
   by Hugo First

What drives a spaceship, fights off enemy aliens, and eats lots of vegetables?

Flash Garden!

Some more books to read in space:
Lasers and Outer Space Weapons
    by Ray Gunn
Where the Stars Are
    by Horace Cope
Taking Off
    by Europe N. Daway
Parachuting from Spaceships
    by Willie Makit
My Life on Pluto
    by I. Malone
A Star Is Born
    by S. Tronomer
Eoop Orrp Ahhrop
    by Marsh Inne
Outer Space Is My Home
    by V. Nus

Rocket Pilot: Mayday! S.O.S.!
Engine on fire! Mayday!
Ground Control: State your
height and position.
Rocket Pilot: Oh, I'm about
five-foot-six and I'm sitting down!

Man: How's business?
Astronomer: It's looking up!

How do aliens from Melmac say good-bye?

ALF-weidersein!